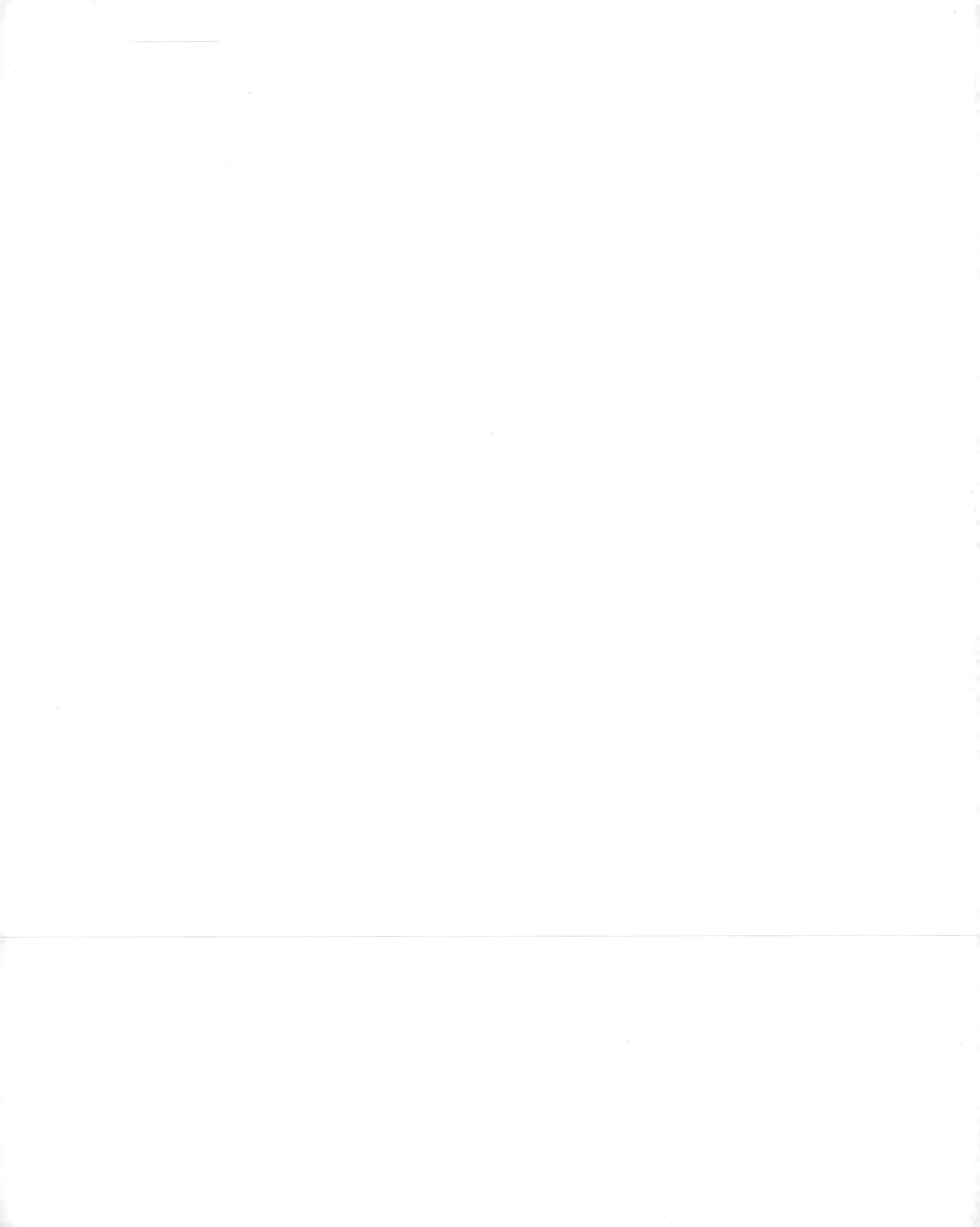

TREEHOUSE LIVING

For Béa

Alain Laurens | Daniel Dufour | Ghislain André | Photographs by Vincent Thfoin

TREEHOUSE LIVING

50 Innovative Designs

Preface by Yann Arthus-Bertrand

ABRAMS, New York

"I watched with the impatience of a child who has been waiting too long."

The day Alain showed me his first designs for treehouses I knew that I would realize a childhood dream that had never left me. As I became older this dream of mine never died—in fact, it only grew, much like the staircase that wound itself around the tree up to a height of 40 feet (12 meters). Up there Ghislain, suspended aloft, was fitting the terrace platform beam by beam, followed by the platform of the treehouse proper. I watched with childlike impatience.

How can I explain my obsession with treehouses? To live in the trees is to have that ideal secret corner, which, for a time, shelters you from everything and everyone. I suppose this has something to do with the small size of the treehouse; ideally it will only accommodate one person, the objects to which he or she is most attached, and some seminal books.

Living up there gives you a sensation of freedom and the benefit of solitude. It is a place of refuge—where I go to seek peace and inspiration.

Yann Arthus-Bertrand

Opposite: Yann Arthus-Bertrand on his way up the staircase to his treehouse.

From left to right: Daniel Dufour, Alain Laurens, and Ghislain André

I awoke telling myself, "I am going to build treehouses."

I had always warned my friends that I would have two lives. It's a simple calculation: Two lives are better than one.

I spent the first life traveling around the world championing the reputations of big brands whose products we consume every day. That job involved constant stress and oppressive responsibility; quickly I sensed that my second life would not be too far off in the horizon.

My second life actually began one day when I awoke from a siesta. I told myself, "I am going to build treehouses." Decision made. What followed has been pure joy: creating our dream with Daniel Dufour, planning and designing our first treehouse, and meeting Ghislain André, a young, brilliant craftsman in wood, whose eyes opened wide when I told him of our plans–it took him just three seconds to decide to join us.

It was a pleasure to find these people who have always wanted to live the outdoor life and rediscover their long-buried sensations of childhood.

With each other we shared so much more than simply constructing treehouses. This is such a beautiful subject!

With this book we hope to showcase our achievements. All of our treehouses were assembled without ever driving a single nail into a tree or cutting a large branch, and the treehouses have been occupied with great discretion–the tree has never been distorted or damaged.

We also want to highlight our inventive, delicate construction methods. The process begins with Daniel's drawings and Ghislain's plans. Each treehouse is then built to measure, taking into account the size of the tree and the layout of its branches.

Finally, this book tells the story of our adventures and the people we have met along the way. Hopefully, by the end, we will have conveyed that small thing known as happiness. If not, our intentions will have failed.

Alain Laurens

A ROUGH-DRAFT TREEHOUSE

This is my treehouse. Ghislain, his father Jean-Marc, and I built it in the same manner as writing a rough draft of a book. We did it this way in order to see, understand, and actualize our dream as it was taking shape before us.

Had I known that this treehouse would be featured in publications the world over, I would have insisted that we finish off the roof with a zinc cover as originally planned. Instead, in keeping to our initial plans, we left this unattractive marine plywood bare. This, however, did not prevent the treehouse from embarking on an international journey.

Region: Lubéron, France

Tree: Aleppo pine

Height: 23 ft. (7 m.)

Treehouse: 81 sq. ft. (7.5 sq. m.)

Terrace: 54 sq. ft. (5 sq. m.)

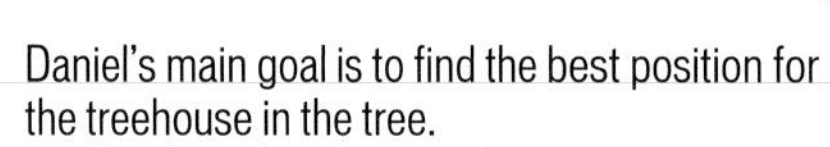

Daniel's main goal is to find the best position for the treehouse in the tree.

Thanks to his photographs of the tree and initial measurements taken from the ground–all accomplished with an infallible eye–he can precisely depict the future treehouse, both inside and out, and render its preliminary plans, in watercolor. This is what we send to our clients.

Once a project has been commissioned, the second phase begins. Ghislain climbs the tree to take more precise measurements. He draws up definitive plans, and the treehouse is built in our workshop. It is then entirely assembled–and dismantled–in the workshop. Finally it is loaded, in pieces, onto a semitrailer and transported to the site.

For this treehouse, which is in a remote, wild location, the staircase has been designed to fit through an opening in the floor, in order to make the entrance more secure.

Above: Hidden in the branches, a lightning conductor protects the treehouse.

Below: The framework of the walls is visible–this treehouse is not insulated.

Opposite: A pulley, rope, and basket can be used to haul up breakfast–or an aperitif.

THE TREEHOUSE AND THE OAK TREE

This was our first commission. Three of us worked on it as snow was falling during the heart of winter. As the days progressed, we watched the staircase wind around the trunk like a lascivious snake.

At a height of 39 feet (12 meters), we reached branches that no one had ever touched–it was like exploring an unknown planet. Four enormous boughs pierce the walls of the treehouse. Inside, the boughs look like statues that have invited themselves into this intimate space. The tree and the treehouse form a whole, as if they had grown together.

Region: Rambouillet Forest, France

Tree: Oak

Height: (treehouse) 39 ft. (12 m.), (terrace) 33 ft. (10 m.)

Treehouse: 75 sq. ft. (7 sq. m.)

Terrace: 108 sq. ft. (10 sq. m.)

Opposite: This spiral staircase winds up to a height of 26 feet (8 meters), ending with a straight 10-foot (3-meter) flight. It consists of two curved stringboards made of glued laminated red cedar.

It is suspended from the trunk by thin quarter-inch (6-mm) cables, and held in position around the trunk by rubber-padded metal bands.

Left: A small staircase leads from the terrace to the treehouse.

Inside are an office, bookshelves, double bed, and even a small twelve-volt radio in one of the drawers under the bed. Electricity is supplied by a solar panel on the roof.

THE TREEHOUSE ON TAHITI BEACH

Set in a large tropical garden, this treehouse looks out toward the sea onto Ramatuelle. The owner is a young grandfather with a swarm of grandchildren; he wanted a special place where he could take refuge. He filled the treehouse with his favorite books and listens to music there. He now spends peaceful days and nights within its walls, coming down only to climb atop a racing bicycle, which again takes him away from the hubbub.

Region: Ramatuelle, Southern France

Tree: Maritime pine

Height: 11 ft. (3.5 m.)

Treehouse: 70 sq. ft. (6.5 sq. m.)

Terrace: 43 sq. ft. (4 sq. m.)

Opposite: With graceful movement, this spiral staircase gently leads you up to the terrace.

Below: The use of metal for the staircase and terrace railings gives the structure a delicate look.

THE GIRLS' TREEHOUSES

This oak is an only child. It has grown alone, without neighbors of comparable size or any competition. It had no need for the frantic race toward light, which stretches trunks of tall, ungainly trees to infinite heights.

As a result, it has an imposing girth and enormous, low boughs, each more inviting as a treehouse venue than the next. For this reason, we decided to build two treehouses.

To help the four girls, for whom these treehouses were built, learn about nature, we engraved the images and names of all the surrounding trees on a panoramic table.

Region:	Geneva, Switzerland
Tree:	Oak
Height:	20 ft. (6 m.)
Treehouse:	75 sq. ft. (7 sq. m.)
Terrace:	108 sq. ft. (10 sq. m.)

The method in which the treehouses are secured to the trees is determined according to the conformation of the tree.

A MUSICAL TREEHOUSE

In Spain's far south, not far from Gibraltar, this treehouse is built on stilts in a handsome cork oak. It was one of our very first treehouses, and it overlooks a magnificent golf course.

For its inauguration, the owner hired an orchestra and invited two hundred friends. She has remained a friend of ours.

Region: Southern Spain

Tree: Cork oak

Height: 10 ft. (3.1 m.)

Treehouse: 83 sq. ft. (7.7 sq. m.)

Terrace: 81 sq. ft. (7.5 sq. m.)

2 m
4 m
2 m 80
2 m
2 m 20
2 m 60

A TREEHOUSE FOR CÉZANNE

This large treehouse on stilts begins with a terrace. Then you reach a second terrace in an oak tree via a footbridge. There, all day long, you can sit and enjoy the view all to yourself. Facing you is Sainte-Victoire Mountain, a mountain much beloved by Cézanne. It changes color almost every hour, from pale gray in the morning mist to blood red at dusk.

Region: Aix-en-Provence, France

Trees: Oak and holm oak

Height: 16 ft. (5 m.)

Treehouse: 43 sq. ft. (4 sq. m.) in the tree

Terrace: 129 sq. ft. (12 sq. m.) on stilts

Opposite: Footbridges–suspended or on stilts–can connect tree to tree, leading right up to a treehouse.

In order to have them blend in even better with the surrounding oaks, all of the load-bearing structures and railings of this project were made from eucalyptus wood rods.

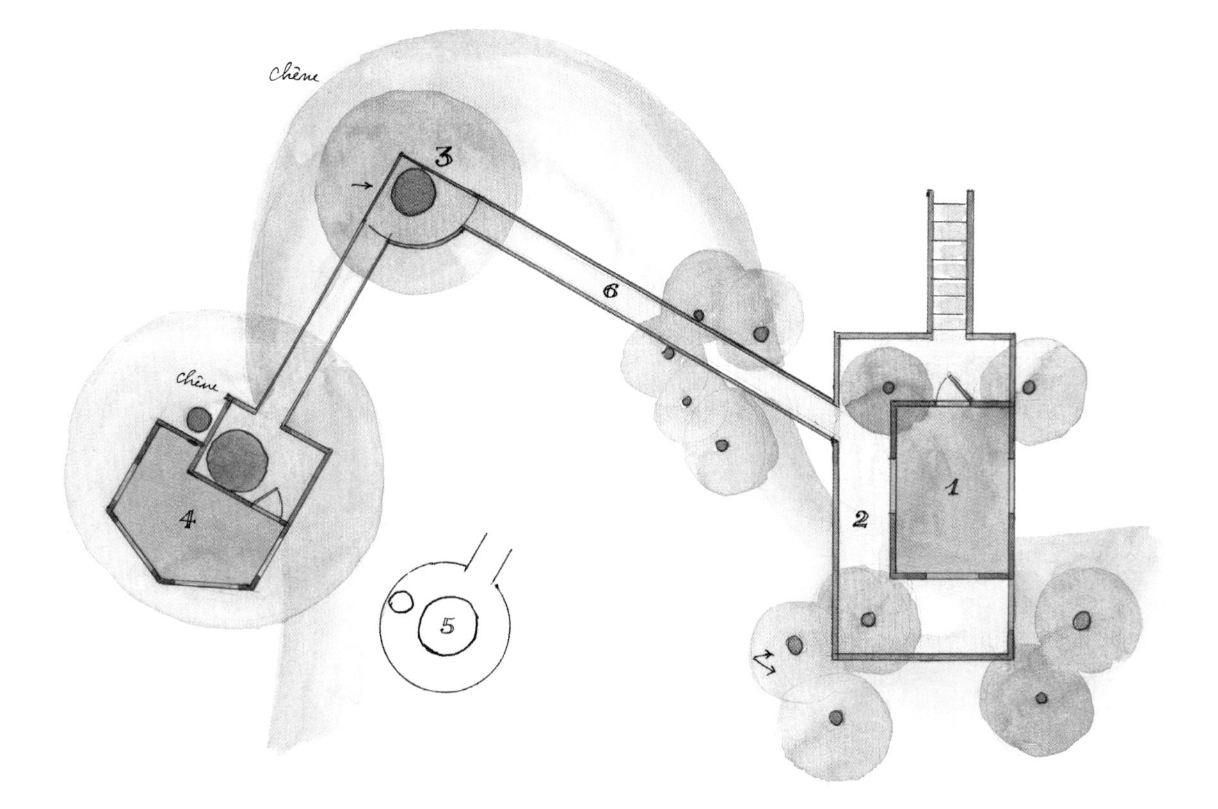
Chêne
3
6
Chêne
1
2
4
5

THE CHAMPAGNE-DRINKER'S TREEHOUSE

We always want to fully understand why people commission treehouses from us. By understanding their reasoning we are better able to create a world that encompasses their dream.

In this particular case, the dream was summed up by one sentence: "I would like a refrigerator with some champagne inside and a treehouse around it." We built the treehouse, perched 36 feet (11 meters) above ground, in a great oak tree in the forest of Rambouillet, with a spiral staircase leading to the "refrigerator." Higher still, a platform overlooks the forest, a great spot for bird-watching.

Region: Rambouillet Forest, France

Tree: Oak

Height: 36 ft. (11 m.)

Treehouse: 108 sq. ft. (10 sq. m.)

Terrace: 32 sq. ft. (3 sq. m.)

Lookout platform: 22 sq. ft. (2 sq. m.)

The lookout platform, at a height of 43 feet (13 meters), is reached via an enclosed ladder on the terrace.

Opposite: When the lower branches of a tree get in the way of a staircase, we use a tree trunk to act as a central pillar and wind the staircase around it.

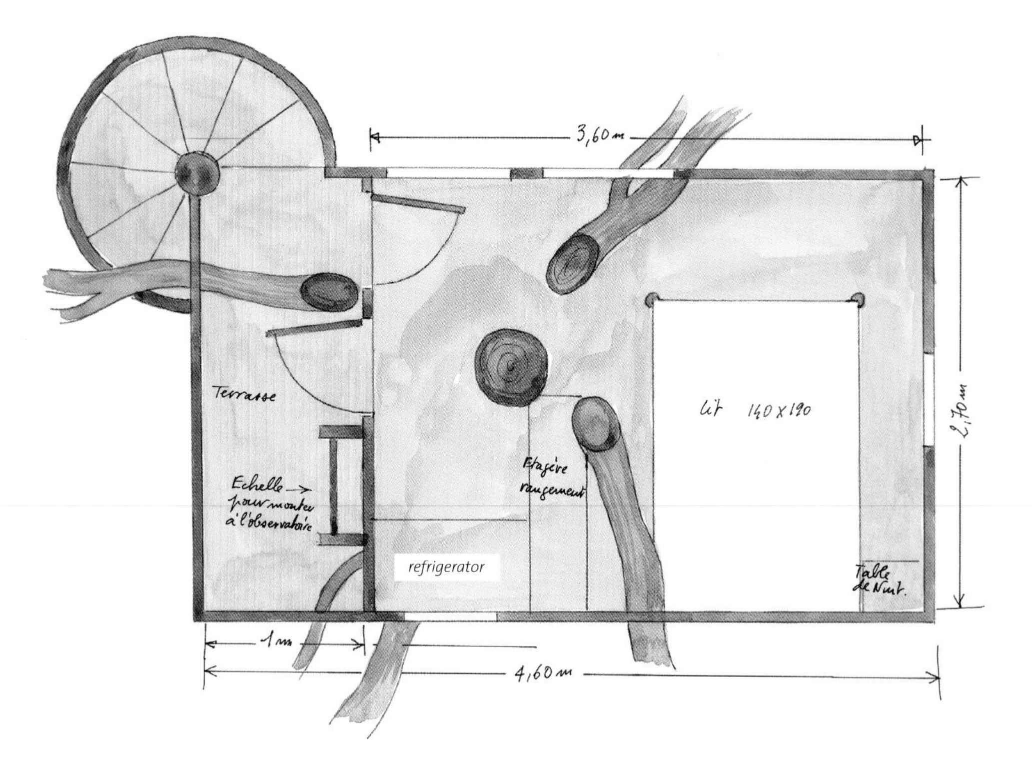

The many boughs that pass through the treehouse's interior make life difficult for us builders. However, we never cut the main branches of a tree that hosts one of our creations.

Above: A large double bed covered with a synthetic thick fur, a sound system, and even a refrigerator, ready to hold champagne.

AN EXOTIC TREEHOUSE

Audrieu, a superb eighteenth-century château, was transformed into a comfortable hotel by its sprightly seventy-year-old owner.

At the front of its gardens, where white tones predominate, two immense, silk-skinned copper beeches tower. Here we perched a treehouse, 36 feet (11 meters) above ground.

Inspired by the original buildings found at parks, this treehouse has some Thai touches; it's inviting, beckoning you to drink a cup of green tea.

Region:	Normandy, France
Tree:	Copper beech
Height:	36 ft. (11 m.)
Treehouse:	75 sq. ft. (7 sq. m.)
Terrace:	129 sq. ft. (12 sq. m.)

In order to climb 36 feet (11 meters), three towers were built on stilts. Each is braced by St. Andrew's crosses.

Note the Thai-style shingles and the railings, which are based on Asian designs.

THE TREEHOUSE AND THE TRUFFLES

This great Aleppo pine stands tall amid fields of truffle oaks. The treehouse and its large terrace look out over the landscape below. In the distance, the Alpilles and the village of Les Baux de Provence are visible. The treehouse's owner, an energetic woman weary of having her truffles stolen, spreads a rumor among the villagers that she has hidden a camera in the treehouse to prevent unscrupulous truffle thieves. The rumor spread fast and the following harvest yielded more truffles than the pervious one. She gratefully invited us for a marvelous truffle dinner.

Region: Lubéron, France

Tree: Aleppo pine

Height: 26 ft. (8 m.)

Treehouse: 86 sq. ft. (8 sq. m.)

Terrace: 86 sq. ft. (8 sq. m.)

In order to lessen the stress on the tree, the spiral staircase was set as far back as possible toward the back of the treehouse.

Left: A fine example of a central bough passing through a treehouse.

Following spread: The door opens onto a large terrace, where the sunset offers a different spectacle every evening.

ÉLÉONORE'S TREEHOUSE

This was our first treehouse on stilts—it leans against a sturdy oak tree. In it you can fall asleep to the sound of crickets and wake up with the sunrise.

The lady of the house is Éléonore, the family's youngest daughter. She knows better than anyone how to listen to nature.

Region: Fayence, France

Tree: Oak

Height: 13 ft. (4 m.)

Treehouse: 65 sq. ft. (6 sq. m.)

Terrace: 65 sq. ft. (6 sq. m.)

Note the curved roof, which gives the treehouse a wide-open view, and the nautical brass porthole.

A TREEHOUSE FOR THE SOFT-HEARTED

From the first time he called me, I got the feeling that I had known him for twenty years; he addressed me informally, with a southern accent and warm words.

At Toulon, a grizzled giant of a man met us at the base of an immense cedar. He wanted to ensconce himself up there to write.

Ghislain built the first curved braces in glued laminated red cedar, which support the treehouse as if it were resting on the petals of a flower.

When the owner returned from a trip, he found his treehouse completed. He called Ghislain and said, "When I got up there, I wept."

Region: Toulon, France

Tree: Cedar

Height: 30 ft. (9 m.)

Treehouse: 86 sq. ft. (8 sq. m.)

Terrace: 54 sq. ft. (5 sq. m.)

Desk, shelves, and a folding bench—the latter is where the exhausted writer can rest.

Above: Note the hinged windows, built offsite in the workshop by our carpenter.

Opposite: To make these curved braces, we produced individual, made-to-measure molds, which were destroyed once they had been used. This technique gives each piece a unique character.

THE EERIE TREEHOUSE

Amidst a small hamlet of houses huddled together on the gentle slopes of the Alps of upper Provence, this treehouse provides an ideal refuge for a frequent traveler.

In front of the houses stands an enormous, thick-set oak, powerful and peaceful. This tree hosts the nest we built for the children: a small treehouse with two beds, one above the other, a table, and a toy chest.

The first time the children tried to spend the night there, they discovered all the strange noises made by the tree. They found the noises so eerie that they soon returned to their bedroom in the house.

Region: Alps of upper Provence, France

Tree: Oak

Height: 10 ft. (3 m.)

Treehouse: 54 sq. ft. (5 sq. m.)

Terrace: 32 sq. ft. (3 sq. m.)

For the children's safety, this staircase has a wide curve, which makes it very easy to climb.

Left: The overhang of the roof over the gables is clearly visible. These slanting edges give the windows effective protection from rain and sun.

THE FLOATING TREEHOUSE

This Austrian pine is gigantic, more than 130 feet (40 meters) high with a girth that commands respect. The trunk of the great tree passes through the center of the treehouse, which is 36 feet (11 meters) above ground. Ghislain decided to suspend the structure using cables. From below the effect is startling: a treehouse that appears to stay aloft by itself, simply impaled on the tree! The spiral staircase winds around the trunk, elegantly rising up to this refuge, which overlooks Lake Geneva.

Region: Salève Mountain, France

Tree: Austrian pine

Height: 36 ft. (11 m.)

Treehouse: 215 sq. ft. (20 sq. m.)

Sixteen feet above the treehouse's roof (63 feet [19 meters] above the ground), a rubber-padded ring is fixed around the trunk. From this ring, cables running down to each corner of the roof bear the treehouse's entire weight. This technique is an alternative to braces supporting the treehouse.

Above: The large windows surrounding the treehouse make it very bright and allow a panoramic view.

Opposite: The absence of braces supporting the platform allows the spiral staircase to lead directly to the treehouse's underside.

THE GIFT-WRAPPED TREEHOUSE

We delivered this treehouse with a great ribbon tied around it in a gigantic bow–just like a present.

All the grandchildren had to do was untie it to find their way into their new playground. We celebrated with the grandparents, toasting the treehouse's completion with champagne. It was a foretaste of Christmas in the trees.

Region: Brittany, France

Tree: Oak

Height: 20 ft. (6 m.)

Treehouse: 75 sq. ft. (7 sq. m.)

Terrace: 65 sq. ft. (6 sq. m.)

A BUCOLIC TREEHOUSE

Right in the middle of Geneva there is a farm, complete with fields and cows. The farmer became a friend and an invaluable ambassador.

A footbridge and a spiral staircase built around a neighboring tree give access to the treehouse. The roof is covered with small wooden hand-cut tiles; the railings are carved; and cows graze on the ground below. We are in Geneva, and at the same time, in the depths of the Swiss countryside.

Region: Geneva, Switzerland

Tree: Maple

Height: 15 ft. (4.5 m.)

Treehouse: 97 sq. ft. (9 sq. m.)

Terrace: 118 sq. ft. (11 sq. m.)

Opposite: We had to make a very precise survey of the site to ensure that this treehouse's platform, cut to size in the workshop, would perfectly fit this cluster of trees. Since it is in the shape of an irregular pentagon, no wall is like the other–each is a different height and set at a different angle.

A JEWEL IN THE SUBURBS

Above the Bois de Vincennes Park, there is a handsome, detached suburban house with a view of Paris. It is home to a globe-trotting grandmother. There was one problem, however. During construction, nothing could be disturbed because her big dog is blind and risked bumping into things should they be moved out of order.

We built a delightful little treehouse in a cluster of hazels. Since then, I have regularly received poems, accounts of journeys, and jars of hazelnuts.

Region: Paris, France	
Tree: Hazel	
Height: 10 ft. (3 m.)	
Treehouse: 43 sq. ft. (4 sq. m.)	
Terrace: 54 sq. ft. (5 sq. m.)	

In order to successfully build a treehouse in hazels, you need to make many sketches of the treehouse. The difficulty lies in achieving a balance between the tree and its guest.

THE BRETON TREEHOUSE

There are two ways of climbing up to heaven: either via a spiral staircase, which loops around four times, or via a 118-foot-long (36-meter-long) suspended footbridge which moves just enough to give you a jolt. And then you reach the treehouse and its terrace, 26 feet (8 meters) above ground. It overlooks an inlet of the Breton sea, at the end of which you can glimpse a charming fishing village. The sunset would bring tears to the eyes of the least sensitive among us.

Region: Brittany, France

Tree: Pine

Height: 26 ft. (8 m.)

Treehouse: 65 sq. ft. (6 sq. m.)

Terrace: 97 sq. ft. (9 sq. m.)

Opposite: Four three-eighths-inch (10 mm) galvanized steel cables support the footbridge. The floor, which consists of 360 planks, is mounted on stainless steel rails, each five feet (1.5 meters) long. The net, three and a half feet (1.1 meters) high, ensures the safety of those adventurers who cross this bridge.

A specially designed metal structure was installed to attach this 118-foot-long (36-meter-long) footbridge to the treehouse platform. Along with being riveted to the platform, it is attached to the ground by cables to counteract the motion exerted by the footbridge.

THE TREEHOUSE OBSERVATORY

The master of the house wanted to look at the stars without the hindrance of the oak tree branches. For this reason, we built a large treehouse—30 feet (9 meters) above ground—resting on six sturdy stilts. The treehouse, glazed throughout, allowed for a 360-degree view: an infinite panorama of villages, hills, and mountains, which can even be observed from the large double bed.

In the evening, he uses a telescope to scan the clear skies above Saint-Michel-de-l'Observatoire.

Never short of ideas, this client also commissioned two delightful treehouses for his daughters, as well as a 197-foot-long (60-meter-long) suspended footbridge across a ravine.

Region:	Alps of upper Provence, France
Tree:	Oak
Height:	30 ft. (9 m.)
Treehouse:	129 sq. ft. (12 sq. m.)
Terrace:	108 sq. ft. (10 sq. m.)

Below: The 360-degree panoramic table shows not only the position of the little hamlet slightly more than a mile (2 km) away but also all of the owner's travels around the world (that table was a real headache, and a labor of love on our part).

Opposite: Six simple stilts 30 feet (9 meters) high (bearing the structure's weight) ensure the stability of this hexagonal platform. Six cables aligned along the structure's main axes brace the treehouse. Each flight of the staircase goes from one stilt to another.

THE TWIN TREEHOUSES

Two sisters needed two treehouses. Though with shared access provided by a bridge adjoining the two houses, each sister has her own tree and her own doll's house for playing mother, nurse, or having doll dinner parties. The braver one could even sleep there. As far as memories go, this is much better than any video game system!

Region: Provence, France
Trees: Oaks
Height: 16 ft. (5 m.)
Treehouse 1: 54 sq. ft. (5 sq. m.)
Treehouse 2: 65 sq. ft. (6 sq. m.)
Terrace: 65 sq. ft. (6 sq. m.)

To make the large platform as light as possible, we used a technique of exerting tension below, which places maximum load on the cables. This allows the sections of the wooden components to be reduced.

THE TERRACE TREEHOUSE

In her great workshop with its large windows, this landscape gardener—queen of gardens—creates, designs, and brings nature to life: exuberant, yet tamed. Her own garden is a veritable spectacle: a whole series of scenes that always offer something new.

In this large plane tree, we built a terrace for her. All she needs to do is climb up to it to be on top of her subject.

Region:	Avignon, France
Tree:	Plane
Height:	13 ft. (4 m.)
Terrace:	86 sq. ft. (8 sq. m.)

Left: Note how the real thing is always faithful to Daniel's design.

Opposite: The covering of the curved string board is made from split logs.

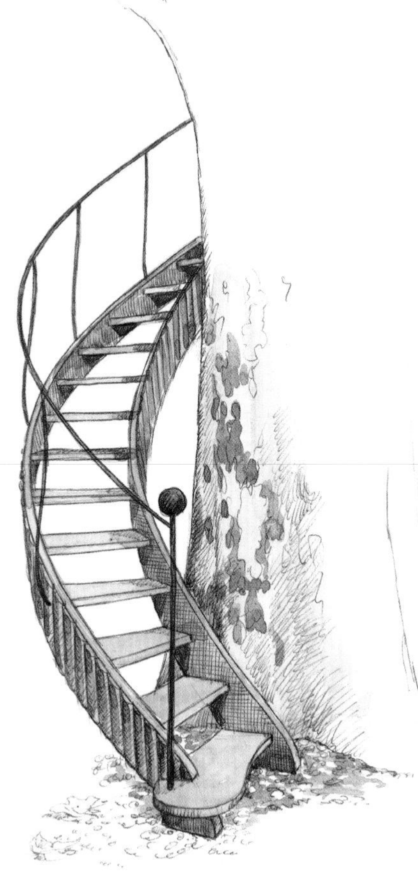

Opposite: The staircase handrail is made of forged iron.

THE ZEN TREEHOUSE

From the terrace of this treehouse, built on stilts between two plane trees, you have a panoramic view of the Alpilles all to yourself. With its foundation buried among the reeds, the treehouse looks as if it is levitating–creating a sense of happiness and serenity.

Region: Alpilles hills, southern France	
Tree: Plane	
Height: 13 ft. (4 m.)	
Treehouse: 65 sq. ft. (6 sq. m.)	
Terrace: 108 sq. ft. (10 sq. m.)	

Above: The thick round posts were inspired by the architecture of the owner's house.

THE TREEHOUSE IN THE CLOUDS

How beautiful it is, and how high!

Atop two giant cypresses, this treehouse and its terrace overlook the sea and the village.

The man who goes up there to write has to climb the fifty-eight steps of the spiral staircase and arrives at the top feeling slightly giddy. There's a brief pause on the terrace to gaze up at the stars, and then there's an attempt to write a few pages without being distracted by the extraordinary view or the night's allure.

Region:	Brittany, France
Tree:	Cypress
Height:	43 ft. (13 m.)
Treehouse:	118 sq. ft. (11 sq. m.)
Terrace:	65 sq. ft. (6 sq. m.)

Left: To build this treehouse, we gathered together and distilled all the knowledge we had acquired in six years and came up with this spiral staircase, which climbs 43 feet (13 meters) around the central trunk and this 118-square-foot (11-square-meter) treehouse ensconced between two giant cypresses.

Opposite: Integrating this treehouse with its setting was especially challenging because we had to thread our way through a veritable forest of branches, many of them dead.

The interior was handled with great care by our carpenter. It features a large desk, generous shelves, and a bench that can be converted into a double bed.

A VERTIGINOUS TREEHOUSE

Under the open sky, this immense maritime pine towers over an olive grove several centuries old, where donkeys graze freely.

Up there—very high indeed—we built a small treehouse that was to be the exclusive refuge of its owner. You access it by climbing a spiral staircase with five coils—you go round and round and finally reach the vertiginous terrace, which dominates the surrounding countryside.

The imposing trunk passes through the treehouse, and you need to squeeze your way past to enter. Once you are in, nothing distracts but the gentle swaying of the wind.

Waking up there at dawn makes you never want to come down again.

Region: The hill country behind Nice, France

Tree: Maritime pine

Height: 39 ft. (12 m.)

Treehouse: 65 sq. ft. (6 sq. m.)

Terrace: 86 sq. ft. (8 sq. m.)

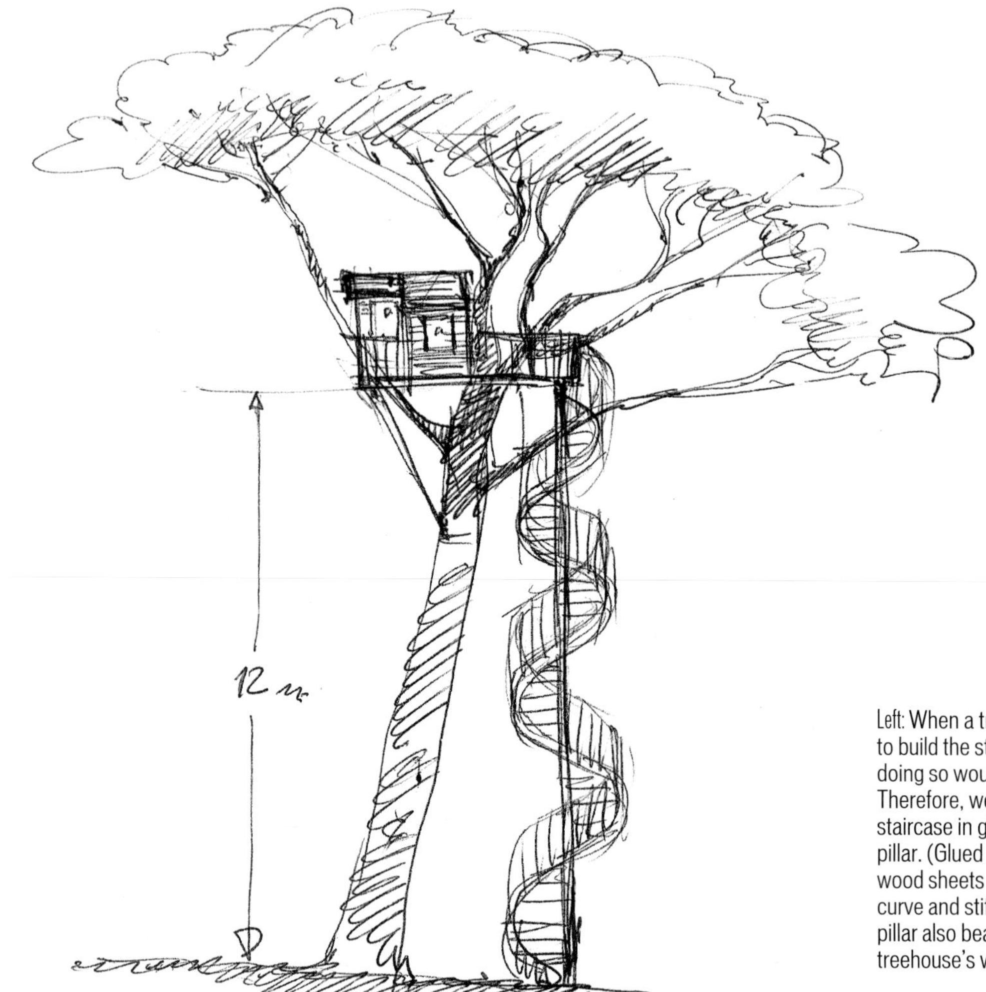

Left: When a tree leans too much, it is not possible to build the staircase around the trunk because doing so would produce a lopsided structure. Therefore, we designed a quintuple-coiled staircase in glued laminated wood with a central pillar. (Glued laminated wood consists of thin wood sheets glued together to form the desired curve and stiffen the structure.) The staircase's pillar also bears a significant proportion of the treehouse's weight.

Below: The curved braces fit between the staircase's central pillar and the string board to ensure the structure is stable and rigid.

A TREEHOUSE WITH VIEWS TO DIE FOR

This garden filled with flowers and trees contains all of the blooms and fruit that nature can produce. This little paradise has only one thing missing: a view of the mountain in the distance. The great oak tree–which is in a perfect location to view the mountain–hosts the treehouse, from whose terrace boasts an unrestricted view of the longed-for landscape.

Region: Alpilles hills, southern France

Tree: Oak

Height: 16 ft. (5 m.)

Treehouse: 97 sq. ft. (9 sq. m.)

Terrace: 129 sq. ft. (12 sq. m.)

Opposite: Curved stilts give the structure a sense of supple movement.

A TREEHOUSE NESTLED IN THE CHILDREN'S PLAYGROUND

La Réserve, in Geneva, is unquestionably the city's finest hotel. It is not only the perfect choice for adults, but it is well suited for children, too.

For the children, we built this large treehouse in a magnificent chestnut tree. They can go there to read, draw, or play; when they want to stretch their legs, a walk along the footbridges through the trees offers a first-class play area. A five-star bedroom in a large cedar tree is now planned for the "older children."

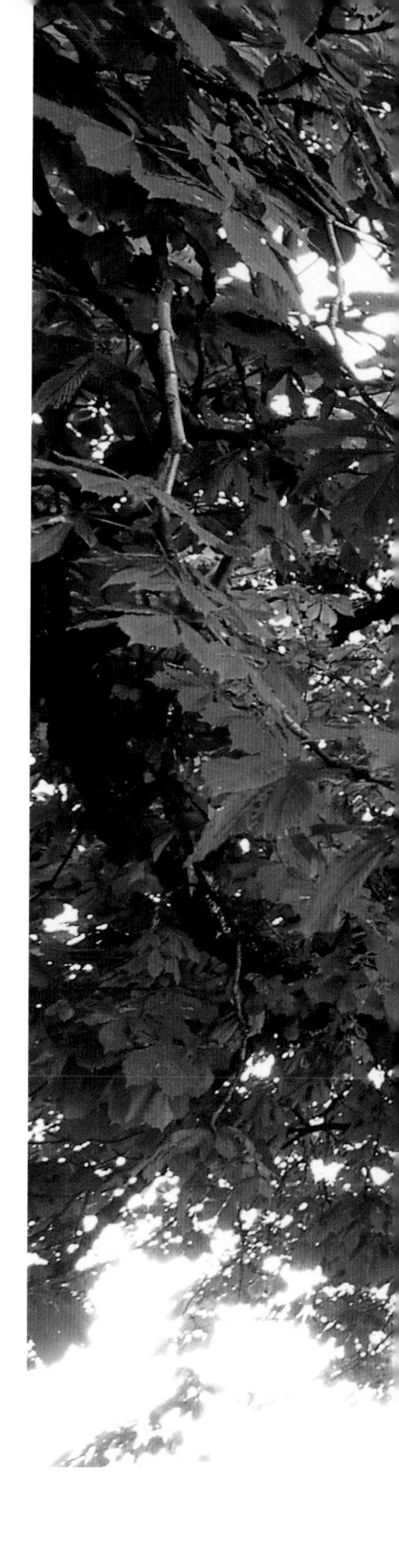

Region: Geneva, Switzerland

Tree: Horse chestnut

Height: 16 ft. (5 m.)

Treehouse: 118 sq. ft. (11 sq. m.)

Terrace: 140 sq. ft. (13 sq. m.)

Note the refinement of these braces under the terrace, which are curved on two planes.

Staircases, suspended bridges, tunnels, and rigid footbridges eventually vanish among the trees before finally leading back to the treehouse, perched in a horse chestnut tree.

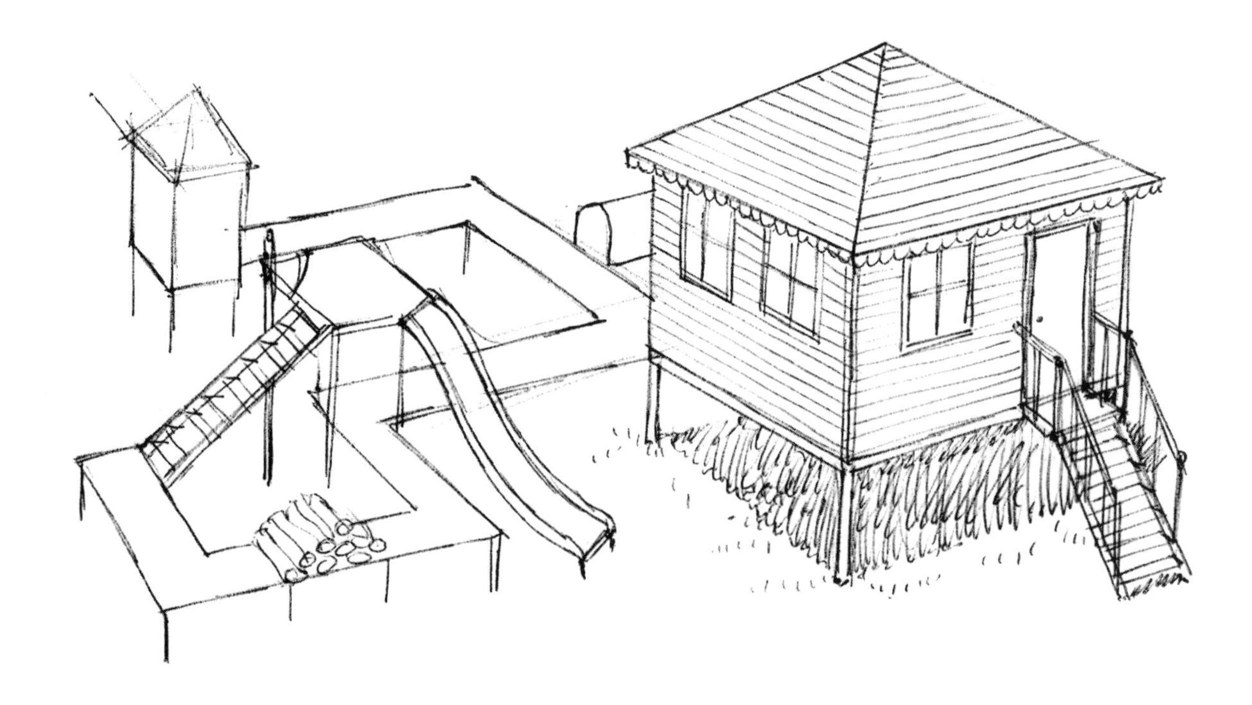

CHATEAUBRIAND'S TREEHOUSE

The arboretum of Vallée-aux-Loups, at Châtenay-Malabry, is a marvel filled with rare, gigantic, strange trees, all wonderfully well cared for. There, you can lose yourself in near solitude. On a street corner, you can climb up to this treehouse and walk over the footbridge, which crosses a delightful stream.

If you want to reread *Mémoires d'outre-tombe* (*Memories from Beyond the Grave*) there, the soul of Chateaubriand, a near neighbor, will follow you on your journey.

Region: Paris area, France

Stilts height: 10 ft. (3 m.)

Treehouse: 118 sq. ft. (11 sq. m.)

Terrace: 86 sq. ft. (8 sq. m.)

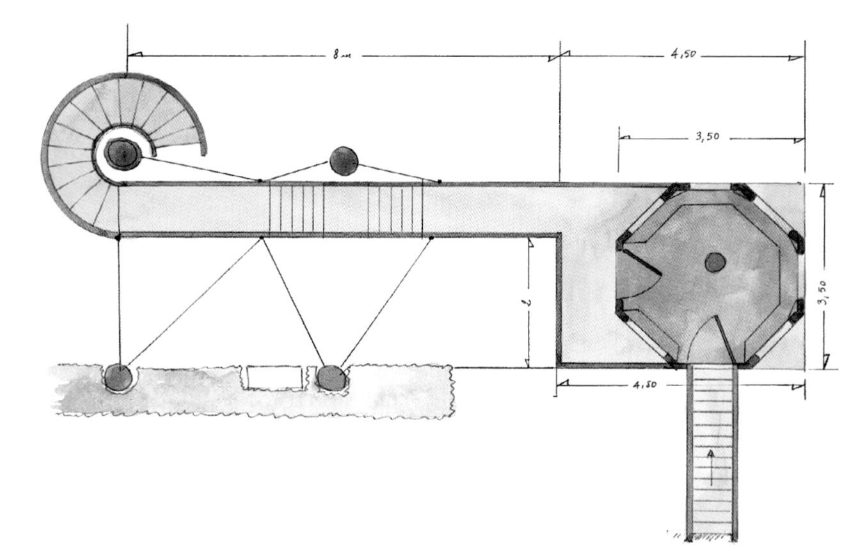

Above: The roof consists of an octagonal wooden frame featuring eight simple ridges. This allows maximum space for the interior.

Opposite: Spruce shingles keep the roof waterproof.

pousse à raser
pousse de larme
pousse superbe

secret
de lune
à mâcher

THE WILD DEERS' TREEHOUSE

We had to wait until the end of mating season before we climbed high into this tree to take the necessary measurements for the treehouse. Here, in the heart of the forest–home to the great stags and hinds–nothing must interfere with their mating.

During construction we saw the deer, from a safe distance, stop by and take a look. After we left, they became used to the treehouse in the great oak tree. Now they come close and pass peaceful hours; during the mating season, their belling is heard for many days and nights.

What the deer won't know is that from the treehouse, a nature lover can be watching them, without disturbing in the slightest the peace of the forest that they live in.

Region: Rambouillet Forest , France

Tree: Oak

Height: 26 ft. (8 m.)

Treehouse: 86 sq. ft. (8 sq. m.)

Terrace: 97 sq. ft. (9 sq. m.)

Opposite: The scaffolding has two functions: It supports the platform before the braces are put in place, and it enables work to be carried out in complete safety, without damaging the tree.

Above: Assembly of the platform structure. Note the openings that allow branches to pass through.

The three main phases of construction:

1. Survey and assessment of the tree.

2. Installation of the platform.

Once the supporting structure is perfectly level, the flooring can be laid down.

The staircase railings and handrail are fixed in place.

A nice hot coffee in the winter sunshine.

At a height of 33 feet (10 meters), you had better be securely harnessed!

3. Constructing and roofing the treehouse.

Tightening of the bolts for the reinforcement of the assembly.

TREEHOUSES THAT STAND GUARD

When we find trees that are not strong enough to support the weight of a treehouse, we use stilts to hold it up. This process consists of fitting the treehouse into the trees, with the trunks passing through the terrace. The illusion is perfect.

Here, at Saint-Paul-de-Vence, the owner's grandson received this Christmas present, a treeehouse nestled in a cluster of oaks, with a view that looks far out to sea.

Region: Saint-Paul-de-Vence, France

Trees: Holm oaks

Height: 13 ft. (4 m.)

Treehouse: 65 sq. ft. (6 sq. m.)

Terrace: 108 sq. ft. (10 sq. m.)

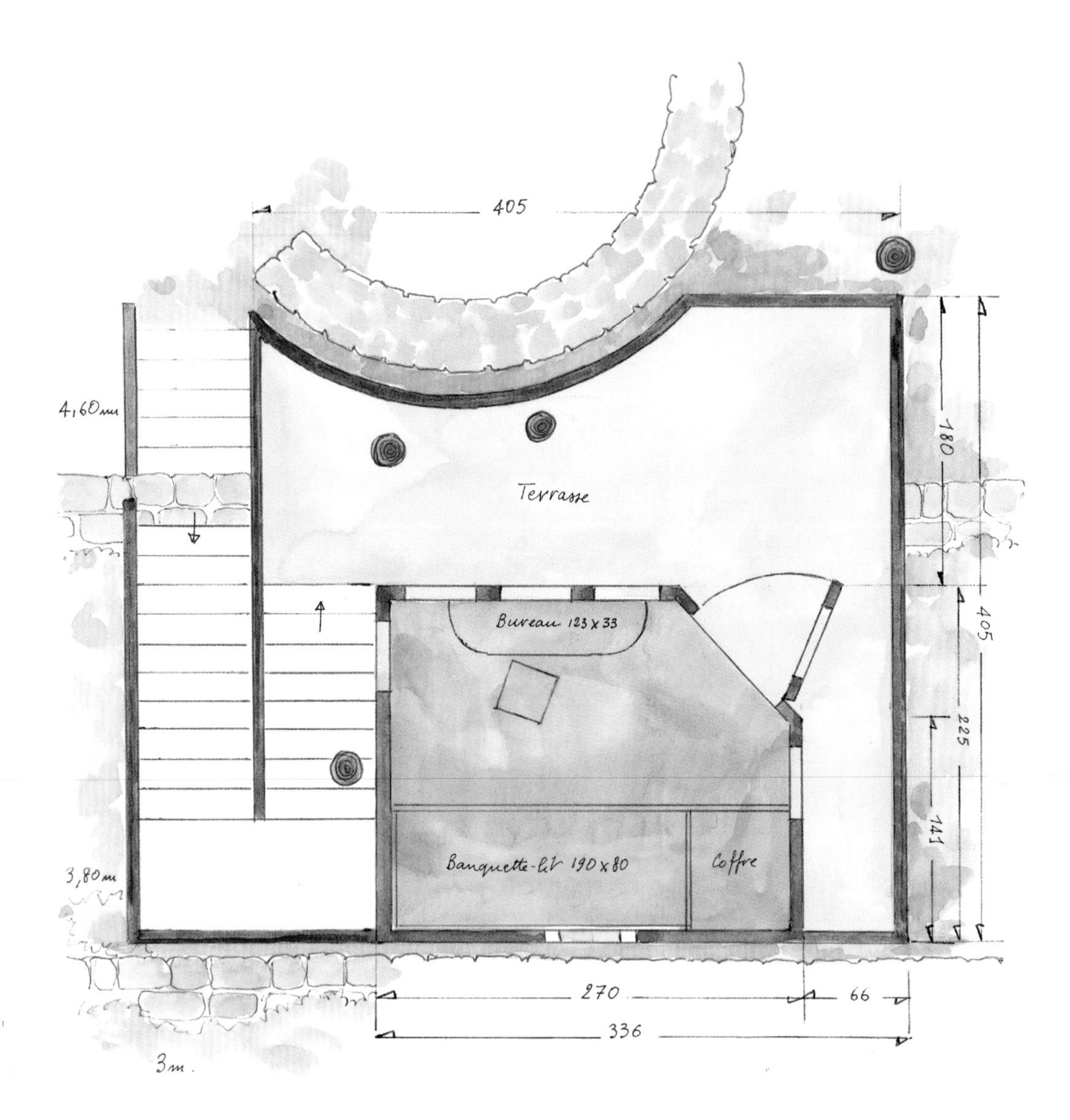

It is always great to draw inspiration from the setting. Here, this curved, low wall gives the terrace a rounded shape.

A CHÂTEAU TREEHOUSE

How can you make four guests comfortable, while simultaneously allowing them to experience the grandeur of the centuries-old trees in the park? By hosting them in a duplex treehouse, of course.

A beautiful elephantine plane tree; a treehouse firmly fixed to its big branches; soft beds; a small bathroom; a generous-sized terrace—what more could you ask for than to spend a few days among the birds?

Region: Aubagne, France

Tree: Plane

Height: 16 ft. (5 m.)

Treehouse: 194 sq. ft. (18 sq. m.)

Terrace: 54 sq. ft. (5 sq. m.)

We raised the treehouse above the thick branches of the plane tree. This was our first duplex treehouse.

THE LOOKOUT TREEHOUSE

Our job is to realize the dreams of those who, as children, built or lived in makeshift treehouses. Sometimes these people give us a little sketch, which we like to use as a jumping-off point.

Here, a Belgian lover of Provence made his own model for a treehouse. It's nestled high in a large oak tree, and its terrace goes virtually all around it, serving as a lookout over the surrounding hills and villages.

The owner, a big, smiling man, spends hours up there working in peaceful silence.

Region: Lubéron, France

Tree: Oak

Height: 23 ft. (7 m.)

Treehouse: 65 sq. ft. (6 sq. m.)

Terrace: 43 sq. ft. (4 sq. m.)

A rigid footbridge, which reaches across from atop a steep bank, gives access to the treehouse.

The owner's model, on which we based our own design.

THE TREEHOUSE OF OUR CHILDHOOD

Three brothers (three musketeers!); a treehouse in a handsome oak tree; a vertical ladder to reach it; a Tyrolean cable that leads to a nearby lime tree; a crenellated tower for attacking and defending; wooden swords; friends; strategies; alliances; battles; tears; laughter; scratches; victors; the vanquished . . . childhood memories are never forgotten. They stay with you for the rest of your life.

Region: Rambouillet Forest, France

Tree: Oak

Height: 13 ft. (4 m.)

Treehouse: 65 sq. ft. (6 sq. m.)

Terrace: 140 sq. ft. (13 sq. m.)

4,50
2 lits superposés
1,65 x 0,66
Bureau
Rangement
3,00
4,00
2,00

Above left and right: You reach this treehouse via an enclosed ladder, which deposits you at the terrace; a gate guards access. Notice the large number of branches that we had to work around in order to install this treehouse.

Top: A gabled porch supported by posts–an extension of the roof–offers protection from the elements.

THE TREEHOUSE IN THE PARK

Climb a spiral staircase built around a neighboring tree and then cross over using a footbridge that leads to this treehouse—although it's a short journey, it's just the right amount of exercise needed before you close the door and plop down on your bed. Now is the perfect time to finish reading your novel or your favorite comic book.

Region: Paris area, France

Tree: Chestnut

Height: 10 ft. (3 m.)

Treehouse: 65 sq. ft. (6 sq. m.)

Terrace: 65 sq. ft. (6 sq. m.)

Opposite and following spread: These photographs show three typical elements of our carpentry work: the staircase curling around the tree trunk, the rigid 16-foot (6-meter) footbridge, and the curved braces in glued laminated red cedar, which provide an elegant but sturdy support for the treehouse.

THE LOVERS' TREEHOUSE

Note to lovers: The Château Valmer Hotel is the first four-star treehouse. The goal was to re-create the comfort found at this luxury hotel at a height of 30 feet (9 meters).

Inside the 172-square-foot treehouse, you'll find a large, soft bed, handsome furniture chosen by the mistress of the house, and a wood-paneled bathroom.

Among the generously proportioned branches of this tree you can eat breakfast late into the morning on the spectacular shaded terrace.

What could be a more ideal place to start your honeymoon, declare your love, or work on a reconciliation?

Region: La Croix-Valmer, France
Tree: Holm oak
Height: 30 ft. (9 m.)
Treehouse: 172 sq. ft. (16 sq. m.)
Terrace: 161 sq. ft. (15 sq. m.)

In this immensely strong tree, we built a luxurious treehouse without supporting posts. All walls are insulated, and the windows are double-glazed. We accomplished this thanks to the sheer size of this tree and to a system that uses a rubber-padded metal collar. This collar, which can be adjusted, ties together all the braces that support the platform.

The pipes providing water and the electrical and telephone lines are hidden, both in the hollowed-out tree trunk and in the staircase's support stilts.

Comfort worthy of a luxury hotel, 30 feet
(9 meters) above ground.

A UNIQUE TREEHOUSE

The ultimate dream is to ascend to your treehouse knowing that you'll be completely alone–no one can follow you and nothing will distract you from your thoughts, your dreams, or your lovemaking.

The secret is the lift. It gently carries you up and deposits you on the terrace. As the sole master of this place, you can choose to watch the deer go by or to have a siesta in your comfortable four-post bed.

Region: Sologne, France

Trees: Oaks

Height: 30 ft. (9 m.)

Treehouse: 129 sq. ft. (12 sq. m.)

Terrace: 151 sq. ft. (14 sq. m.)

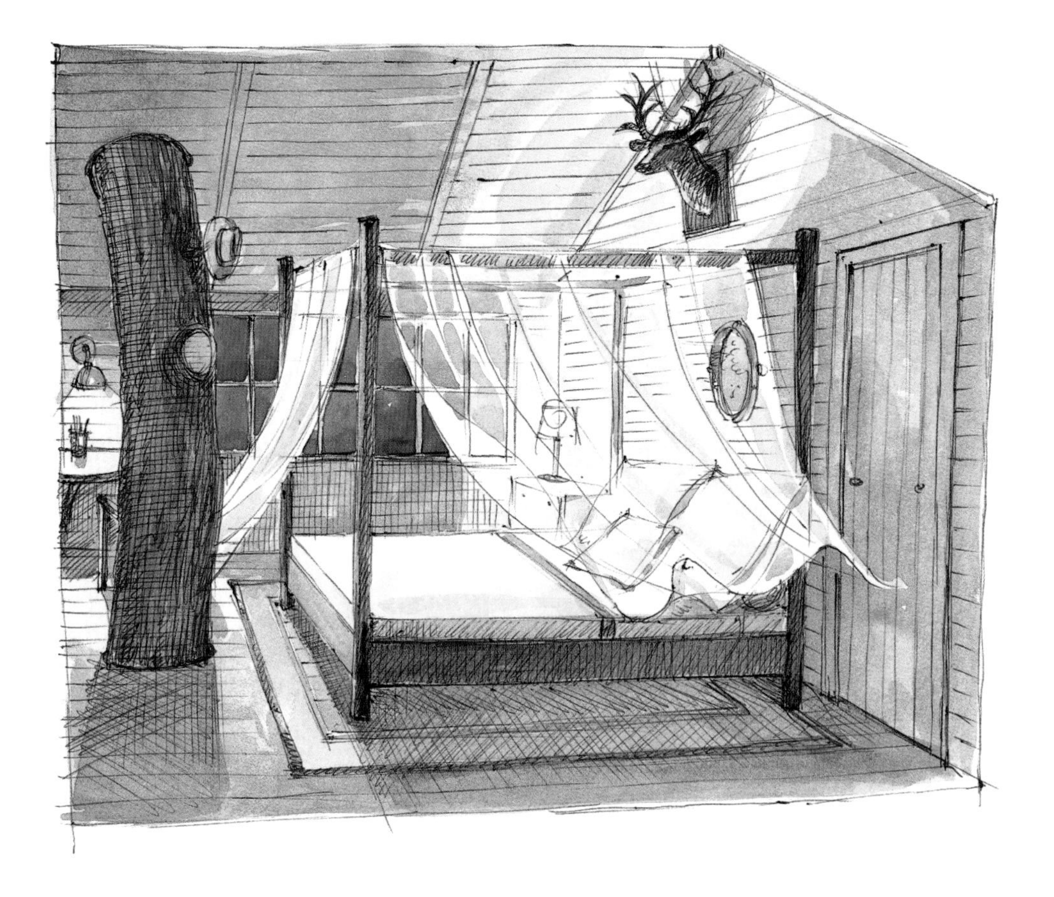

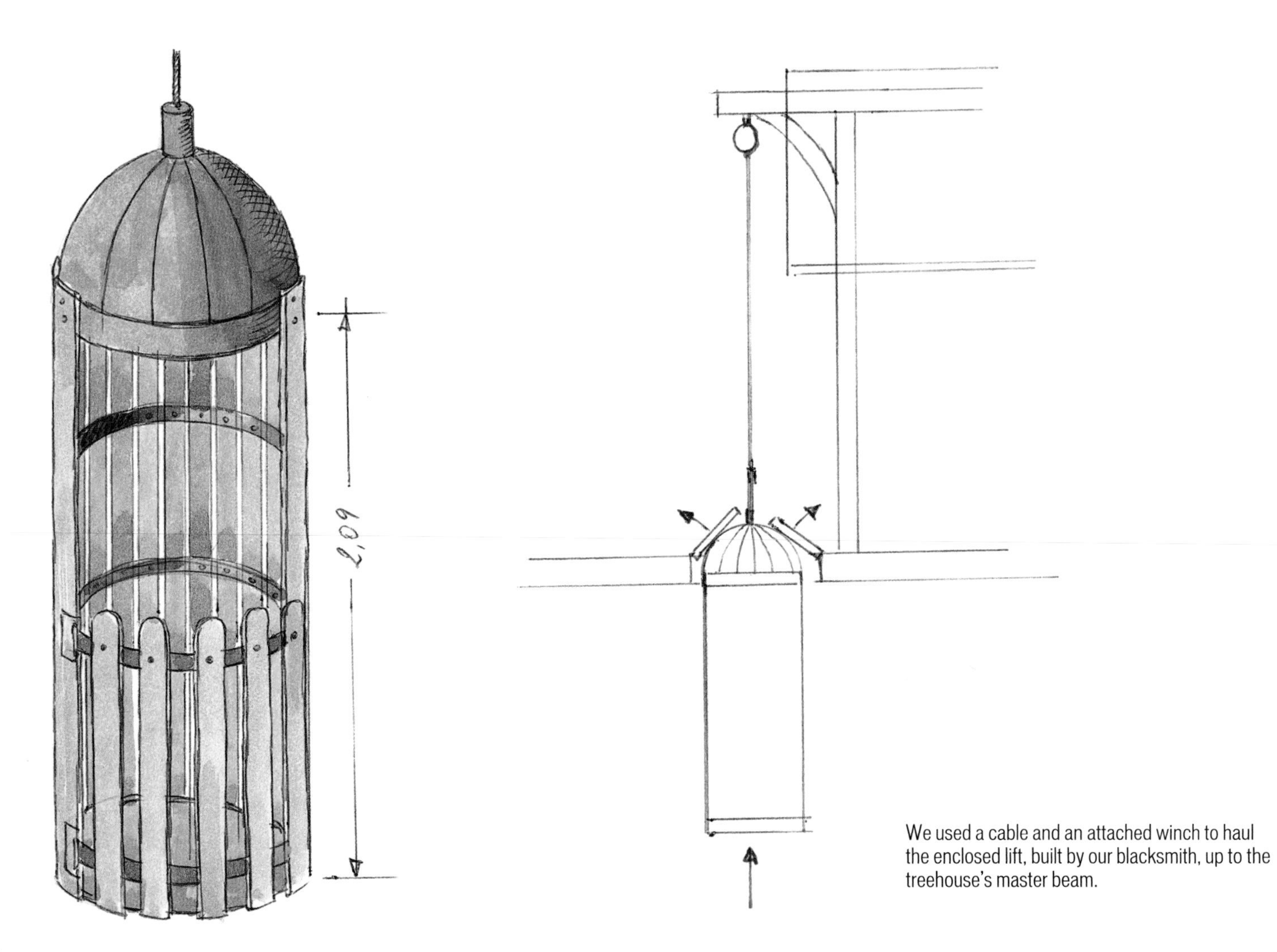

We used a cable and an attached winch to haul the enclosed lift, built by our blacksmith, up to the treehouse's master beam.

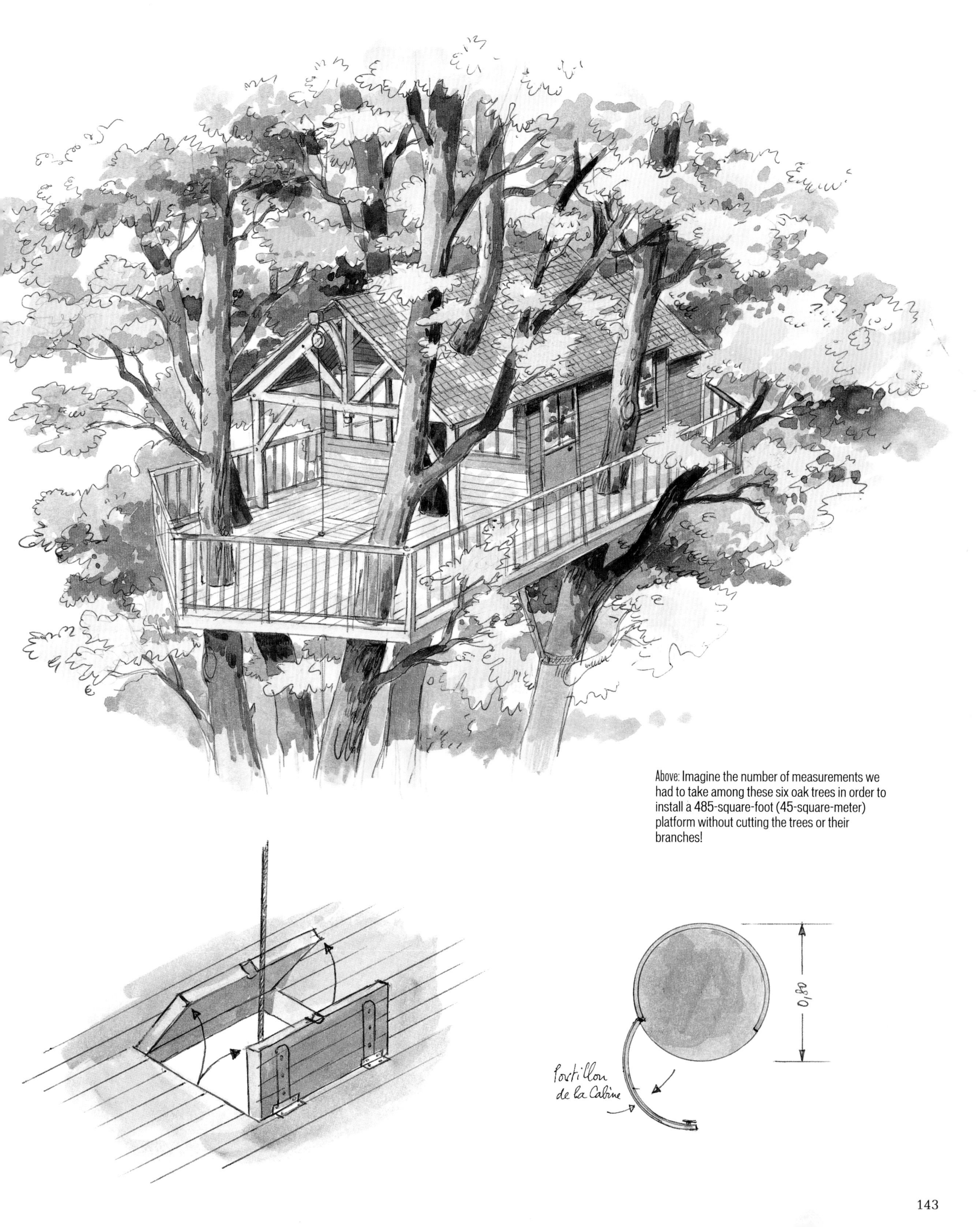

Above: Imagine the number of measurements we had to take among these six oak trees in order to install a 485-square-foot (45-square-meter) platform without cutting the trees or their branches!

A TREEHOUSE FOR ALL

Grown-ups who have treehouses built for their children or grandchildren often say to us, "Make the beds a bit on the large side, you never know. . ." or "Build that a little bigger, in case one day. . ."

In this treehouse, it is not unusual to see family and friends drinking aperitifs in the sun, while the children wait their turn to take over.

Region: The hill country near Nice, France

Tree: Oak

Height: 13 ft. (4 m.)

Treehouse: 65 sq. ft. (6 sq. m.)

Terrace: 108 sq. ft. (10 sq. m.)

The roof is a square-based pyramid, with four equal sloping surfaces.

Left: To keep the curious at bay, a staircase leads directly beneath a trapdoor that opens onto the terrace.

A SECRET TREEHOUSE

A handsome oak like this one is ideal for a treehouse, even though its lower branches were a headache for the carpenters when they installed the spiral staircase.

At 26 feet (8 meters) above ground, the treehouse is well situated among the tree's generously proportioned branches. In spring, the treehouse disappears completely among the foliage.

Region: La Garde-Freinet, southern France
Tree: Oak
Height: 26 ft. (8 m.)
Treehouse: 86 sq. ft. (8 sq. m.)
Terrace: 86 sq. ft. (8 sq. m.)

Opposite: Here is yet another example of a staircase winding around the trunk and threading its way among the branches.

Below: The railings were made from small split eucalyptus logs.

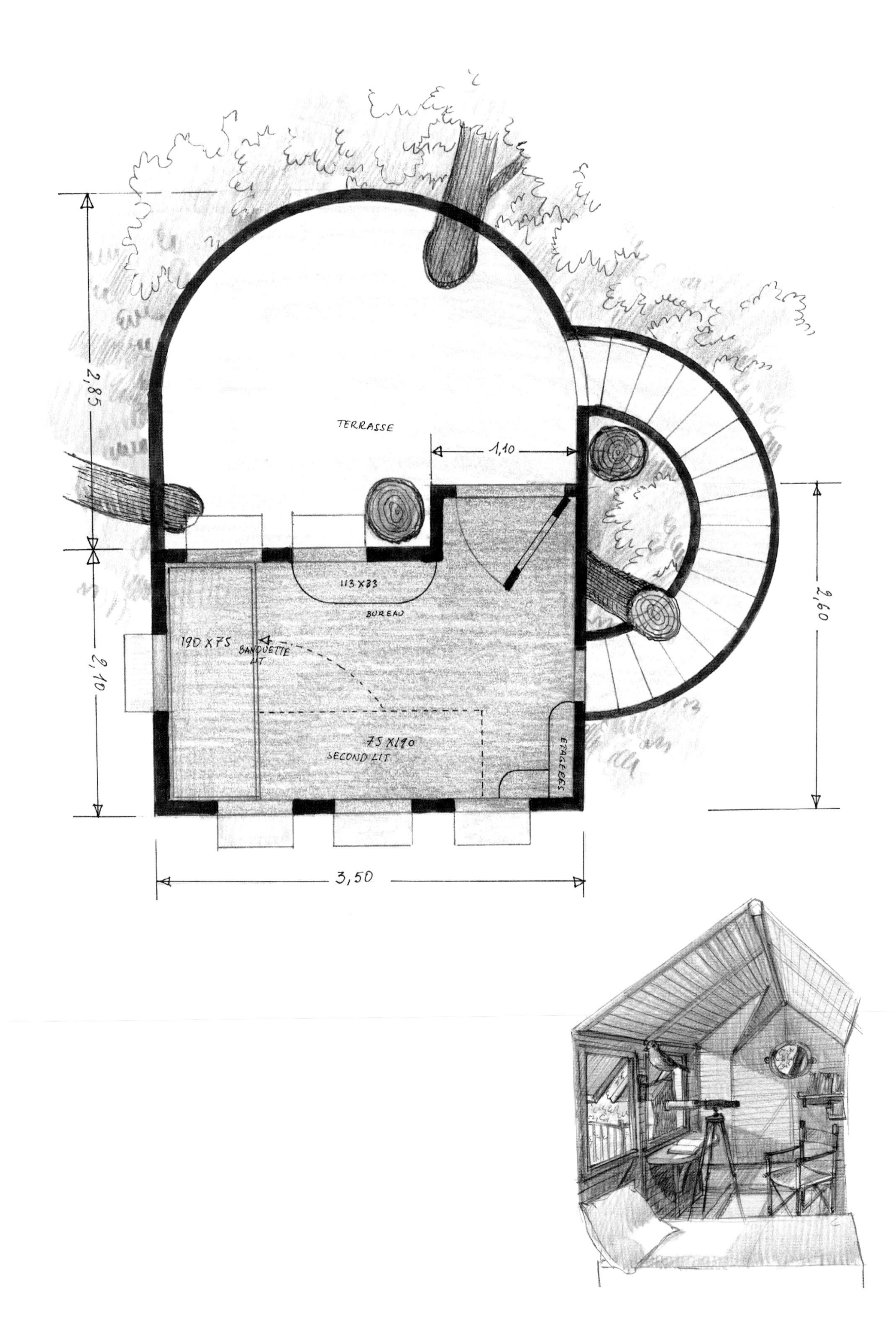

TERRASSE
1,10
2,85
113 X 33
BUREAU
190 X 75
BANQUETTE LIT
2,10
75 X 190
SECOND LIT
ETAGERES
2,60
3,50

This is a fine example of a treehouse being constructed without a single branch being cut–a perfect marriage of respect and innovation. For this to happen, we must spend a long time in the tree and take extremely precise measurements. As a result, the treehouse that has been built in the workshop will fit perfectly when reassembled.

THE HOLIDAY TREEHOUSE

Many people dream of spending a night in a treehouse. The hundreds of telephone calls we have received over the last few years asking for that gave us the idea of offering treehouses for guests. The pioneer of this idea was Diane van den Berge in Saint-Paul-de-Vence. This treehouse was so successful–helped along by Diane's dazzling smile–that we built three more.

Hidden in pretty little woods, the treehouses overlook a large swimming pool; the water found therein is filtered entirely by plants.

Region: Saint-Paul-de-Vence, France

Stilts height: 16 ft. (5 m.)

Treehouse: 183 sq. ft. (17 sq. m.)

Terrace: 108 sq. ft. (10 sq. m.)

Following spread: In this treehouse, a highly compact layout successfully displays a large bedroom, a bathroom, and a huge terrace.

THE TREEHOUSE REFUGE

This small treehouse has no prominent façade. In southern France, the weather is so pleasant at night that the owner, an indefatigable builder, decided to leave the treehouse open to the immense panorama overlooking the sea. He put his telescope up there to look at the stars; a comfortable armchair helps him read in peace.

Region: Cannes, France
Tree: Oak
Height: 13 ft. (4 m.)
Treehouse: 65 sq. ft. (6 sq. m.)
Terrace: 75 sq. ft. (7 sq. m.)

THE SAVAGE'S TREEHOUSE

The fortunate "green" owner of this treehouse–a tireless traveler, an habitué of the great open spaces, and an ecologist at heart–has done such a magnificent job furnishing it that he often forsakes his comfortable house nearby. After all, it's far easier up there to partake in one of his favorite pastimes: counting shooting stars.

Region: Provence, France

Stilts height: 16 ft. (5 m.)

Treehouse: 118 sq. ft. (11 sq. m.)

Terrace: 118 sq. ft. (11 sq. m.)

Above: Thick bedclothes make it possible to sleep in an uninsulated treehouse in all types of weather.

THE DUPLEX TREEHOUSE

Sitting at the edge of a forest, this treehouse allows its occupants to observe wildlife and passing equestrians.

Originally, this project had been intended for the owner's children and future grandchildren. As the project evolved, however, the parents couldn't resist–they wanted a love nest on the upper floor. A large work area, in front of a long window, is the place where the children draw and the parents with portable computer in hand plan their future garden.

Region: Normandy, France

Stilts height: 10 ft. (3 m.)

Treehouse: 344 sq. ft. (32 sq. m.), encompassing two floors

Terrace: 140 sq. ft. (13 sq. m.)

THE TREEHOUSE BY THE DUCK POND

It could very well be a picture-postcard image: a great pine tree on the bank of a small pond filled with ducks. This 13-foot (4-meter) treehouse was made for the owner's children. It has a 360-degree view of the forest; from it one can see does, stags, rabbits, hares, and, of course, all the birds imaginable.

Region: Rambouillet Forest, France

Tree: Pine

Height: 13 ft. (4 m.)

Treehouse: 65 sq. ft. (6 sq. m.)

Terrace: 54 sq. ft. (5 sq. m.)

Opposite: Note the long staircase, which, in one flight, reaches the treehouse. Two gates ensure that the children are safe.

THE WATCHTOWER

Region: Alpilles hills, Southern France
Height: 26 ft. (8 m.)
Terrace: 129 sq. ft. (12 sq. m.)

On the perimeter wall of an abbey, in the heart of the Alpilles, we built this watchtower, which boasts far-reaching views. Its flag, flying 46 feet (14 meters) in the air, alerts lost travelers that other living souls are nearby; the treehouse towers above the abbey's superb gardens. This was a magnificent display of style and a matter of pride for the carpenters—they built a technically complex structure.

As the months passed, the wood became silvery gray, taking on the color of the stone wall. Thus, the tower looks as if it has always been there; it both allows enemies to be spotted and welcomes friends.

This project demanded a lot of prep work: Along with the time-consuming drawings, the wood components needed to be prepared and cut. Once at the actual site, the assembly of the treehouse was made much easier by the meticulousness and precision of the operations carried out in the workshop.

A FAMILY TREEHOUSE

This is a holiday treehouse for peaceful family vacations. The large treehouse is for the grown-ups; the small one is for the children—hooray for holidays!

From the terrace of the large treehouse a footbridge leads to another small treehouse, which has two bunk beds. In the evening, the parents have quiet time, while the children have their share of adventure.

Region: Saint-Paul-de-Vence, France
Stilts height: 16 ft. (5 m.)
Treehouse: 183 sq. ft. (17 sq. m.)
Terrace: 108 sq. ft. (10 sq. m.)

THE CHILDREN'S WORLD

This small treehouse, perched atop a large pine tree, is exclusively reserved for the many children who use it. When they take possession of such a special place, they quickly make it their own and invent all sorts of games–this is their world, far from the adults. While in the treehouse they acquire true independence.

Region: Saint-Tropez, France
Tree: Stone pine
Height: 23 ft. (7 m.)
Treehouse: 65 sq. ft. (6 sq. m.)
Terrace: 65 sq. ft. (6 sq. m.)

This treehouse is located in the middle of a pinewood forest overlooking the bay of Saint-Tropez.

Opposite: The trapdoor is mounted on jacks, which makes it easier to open.

THE SPORTSMAN'S TREEHOUSE

For purists, or the most sporting-minded, we offer access to treehouses via an enclosed ladder. Generously sized uprights, stainless steel rungs, and 180-degree protection offer the most direct route of access. This one climbs more than 30 feet (9 meters) to reach a very beautiful treehouse, which overlooks the Champagne countryside.

The good news: You can rent it!

Region: Champagne-Ardennes, France

Tree: Oak

Height: 30 ft. (9 m.)

Treehouse: 75 sq. ft. (7 sq. m.)

Terrace: 32 sq. ft. (3 sq. m.)

A small gate at the lower end of the ladder keeps out unwanted visitors.

THE FARMHOUSE TREEHOUSE

In the heart of Brittany, on an attractive, busy farm where, among other things, Percheron horses are bred, this treehouse can comfortably accommodate four people. Whether up at the cock's crow or sleeping in late, breakfast here is always wonderful.

Region: Brittany, France

Tree: Walnut

Height: 10 ft. (3.2 m.)

Treehouse: 280 sq. ft. (26 sq. m.)

Terrace: 145 sq. ft. (13.5 sq. m.)

A CINEMATIC TREEHOUSE

Here in Brittany, there is a mill, a river, and a treehouse that towers over this exceptional spot. This is the first treehouse we have placed on a rock. Inaccessible at first, we had to clear a route, build a footbridge that skirted around the rock, and install the entire structure atop the rock, facing the rising sun.

On the terrace—when the urge strikes—you can enjoy a late breakfast or a few delicious oysters from Riec-sur-Belon (best washed down with Muscadet).

Region: Brittany, France

Rock height: 23 ft. (7 m.)

Treehouse: 129 sq. ft. (12 sq. m.)

Terrace: 65 sq. ft. (6 sq. m.)

Above: The footbridge that winds around the rock and the treehouse are fixed to the granite by metal expander bolts.

THE PEACEFUL TREEHOUSE

On a large, wild, and very well kept estate in the Sologne region, every oak tree you see beckons you to build a treehouse in it.

This oak tree overlooks a huge pool inhabited by myriad birds, including large numbers of ducks. The treehouse—well ensconced in the heart of the tree—is both a place where you can watch wildlife and a hideaway where you can spend the night; it's a perfect spot to watch the sunrise, too.

Region: Sologne, France

Tree: Oak

Height: 30 ft. (9 m.)

Treehouse: 86 sq. ft. (8 sq. m.)

Terrace: 108 sq. ft. (10 sq. m.)

Opposite: This staircase features a triumvirate of construction types: a curved staircase with two string boards, a curved staircase around a central pillar, and a straight staircase with two short flights.

A BED IN THE SKY

We designed the "Bed in the Sky" for all those who love life in the trees.

Some people don't have access to large trees; others don't have the budget to build a treehouse. The "Bed in the Sky" can be installed even in medium-sized trees, measuring up to 33 feet (10 meters) above ground. A comfortable mattress (one that can withstand damp evenings) measures 22 square feet (2 by 2 meters) and welcomes you for a night under the stars.

Lying under the duvet, it is easy to imagine one is Italo Calvino's baron in the trees: "The moon rose late, and shone above the branches. In their nests slept the titmice, huddled up like him."

Region: Lubéron, France

Tree: Aleppo pine

Height: 26 ft. (8 m.)

Bed: 54 sq. ft. (5 sq. m.)

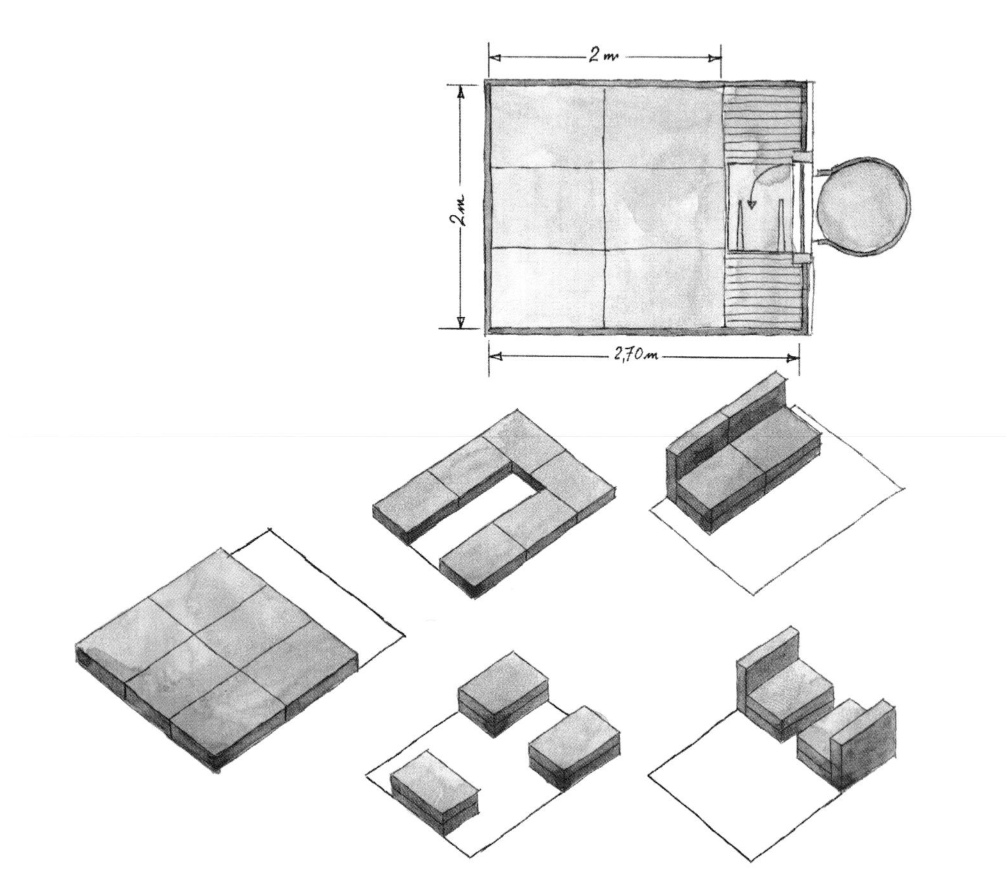

Left: The mattress is made up of six cushions. They can be arranged to form a couch, armchairs, or poufs, enabling the "Bed in the Sky" to be used during the day.

Opposite: The "Bed in the Sky" places almost no demands on the tree. It bears its own weight, which is supported entirely by the uprights of the ladder. The tree merely props up the structure.

THE BAMBOO TREEHOUSE

This particular treehouse represented our desire to use bamboo, according to traditional principles. We wanted to offer this kind of structure to those who might appreciate a treehouse with an Asian flavor. With Gerry Langlais, an architect who specializes in bamboo, it was no sooner said than done. Enthusiasts, take note!

Region: Lubéron, France

Tree: Oak

Height: 20 ft. (6 m.)

Treehouse: 118 sq. ft. (11 sq. m.)

Terrace: 54 sq. ft. (5 sq. m.)

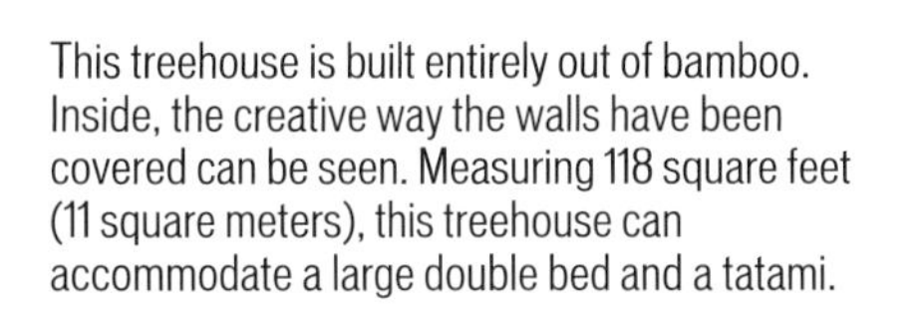

This treehouse is built entirely out of bamboo. Inside, the creative way the walls have been covered can be seen. Measuring 118 square feet (11 square meters), this treehouse can accommodate a large double bed and a tatami.

THE WORKSHOP

From left to right:

Front row: Ghislain André, Nicolas Moreau, Bettina Bauer, Constand Deiana, Aimé Baret

Back row: Pierre Nègre, Alain Laurens, Daniel Dufour

Missing: Matthieu Adamski

Opposite, top: A view of the entire workshop. The joists of a treehouse are in the foreground, next to the swinging crosscut saw. In the background, you see the area where curved staircases are made; to the right is the carpentry area.

Opposite, bottom right: Glued string boards with grooves, ready for the steps.

Above: Gluing mold for bending string boards, used for making curved staircases.

Opposite: String boards just removed from the mold.

RESOURCES

Page 34. An Exotic Treehouse.
Château d'Audrieu (Château hotel)
M. Gérard Livry Level
14250 Audrieu
France
+33 2 31 80 21 52
www.chateaudaudrieu.com
(Treehouse not for rent)

Page 82. The Terrace Treehouse.
Dominique Lafourcade, landscape gardener
Studio Bruno et Alexandre Lafourcade
10, bd Victor-Hugo
13210 Saint-Rémy-de-Provence
France
+33 4 90 92 10 14
(Treehouse not for rent)

Page 100. A Treehouse Nestled in the Children's Playground.
HMC Hôtel La Réserve
301, route de Lausanne
1293 Bellevue
Switzerland
+41 22 959 59 59
www.lareserve.com
(Treehouse not for rent)

Page 104. Chateaubriand's Treehouse.
Arboretum de la Vallée-aux-Loups
46, rue de Chateaubriand
92290 Châtenay-Malabry
France
(Park can be visited, but treehouse not for rent)

Page 120. A Château Treehouse.
Château des Creissauds
M. Guillaume Ferroni
Le Clos Rufisque
13400 Aubagne
France
+33 4 91 24 88 69
www.chateaudescreissauds.com
(Treehouse for rent)

Page 134. The Lovers' Treehouse.
Hôtel Château Valmer
84420 La Croix-Valmer
France
+33 4 94 55 15 15
www.chateauvalmer.com
(Treehouse for rent)

Page 154. The Holiday Treehouse.
Page 178. A Family Treehouse.
Orion Bed and Breakfast
Diane van den Berge
2436 Chemin du Malvan
06570 Saint-Paul-de-Vence
France
+33 6 75 45 18 64
www.orionbb.com
(Treehouse for rent)

Page 186. The Sportsman's Treehouse.
Château du Mont Remy
52300 Nomécourt
France
+33 6 07 53 19 70
www.chatnom.com
jacques.montremy@wanadoo.fr
(Treehouse for rent)

Page 188. The Farmhouse Treehouse.
Les Écuries de Kerbalan
Brigitte and Joëlle Vincent
22290 Gommenech
France
+33 2 96 52 32 11
www.perso.wanadoo.fr/brigitte.vincent
(Treehouse for rent)

Additional resources:

Le Parc Mont Oz Arbres
La Gallinée Route d'Espagne
066230 Prat-de-Mollo
France
www.montozarbres.com
(Treehouse for rent)

Le Parc Arborigène
In the Parc Régional de la Montagne de Reims,
near Faux de Verzy
The Champagne-Drinker's Treehouse
51380 Verzy
France
+33 6 89 44 73 68 (Olivier Couteau)
www.arborigene.com
(Champagne tasting inside the treehouse)

Agriturismo La Piantata
Strada Provinciale Arlenese
01010 Arlena di Castro (Viterbo)
Italy
+39 335 604 96 30 (Renzo Stucchi)
agriturismo@lapiantata.it
(Treehouse for rent)

Le parc Botanique du Château de Suscinio
29600 Morlaix-Ploujean
France
+33 2 98 72 05 86
www.agglo.morlaix.fr
(Treehouse not for rent)